W9-CUD-195

U.S.A. TRAVEL GUIDES

WEST VIRGINIA

BY ANN HEINRICHS • ILLUSTRATED BY MATT KANIA

Published by The Child's World®
1980 Lookout Drive • Mankato, MN 56003-1705
800-599-READ • www.childsworld.com

Photo Credits
Photographs ©: Jon Bilous/Shutterstock Images, cover, 1, 15; iStockphoto, 7, 31; bobistraveling CC2.0, 8; Carol M. Highsmith/Carol M. Highsmith Archive/Library of Congress, 11, 16, 28; Noelle CC2.0, 12; Jim Lo Scalzo/EPA/Newscom, 19; Ron Cogswell CC2.0, 20; Vicki Smith/AP Images, 23; Zack Frank/Shutterstock Images, 24; Jay Romanceles/Shutterstock Images, 27; Lori Wolfe/The Herald-Dispatch/AP Images, 32; USFWS, 35; Shutterstock Images, 37, 38

ISBN 9781503819887
LCCN 2016961626

Printing
Printed in the United States of America
PA02334

Ann Heinrichs is the author of more than 100 books for children and young adults. She has also enjoyed successful careers as a children's book editor and an advertising copywriter. Ann grew up in Fort Smith, Arkansas, and lives in Chicago, Illinois.

About the Author
Ann Heinrichs

Matt Kania loves maps and, as a kid, dreamed of making them. In school he studied geography and cartography, and today he makes maps for a living. Matt's favorite thing about drawing maps is learning about the places they represent. Many of the maps he has created can be found in books, magazines, videos, Web sites, and public places.

About the
Map Illustrator
Matt Kania

On the cover: Looking for scenic mountain views?
Ride a train along the mountains in Harpers Ferry.

OUR WEST VIRGINIA TRIP

WEST VIRGINIA

Let's take a trip through West Virginia! You'll find it's a great place to explore.

You'll hike up mountains and wander through forests. You'll go deep down into a coal mine. You'll hear fiddlers and visit logging camps. You'll see a gigantic radio telescope. You'll watch glassblowers make glass. And you'll eat all the pasta you can hold!

How's that for a fun trip? Are you ready to roll? Then buckle up and hang on tight. It's time to hit the road!

WELCOME TO WEST VIRGINIA

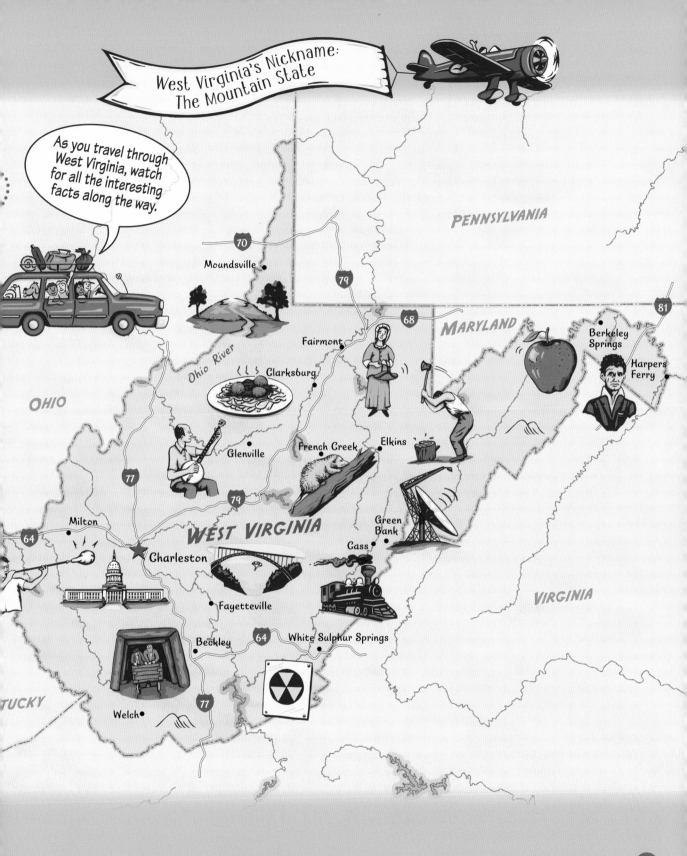

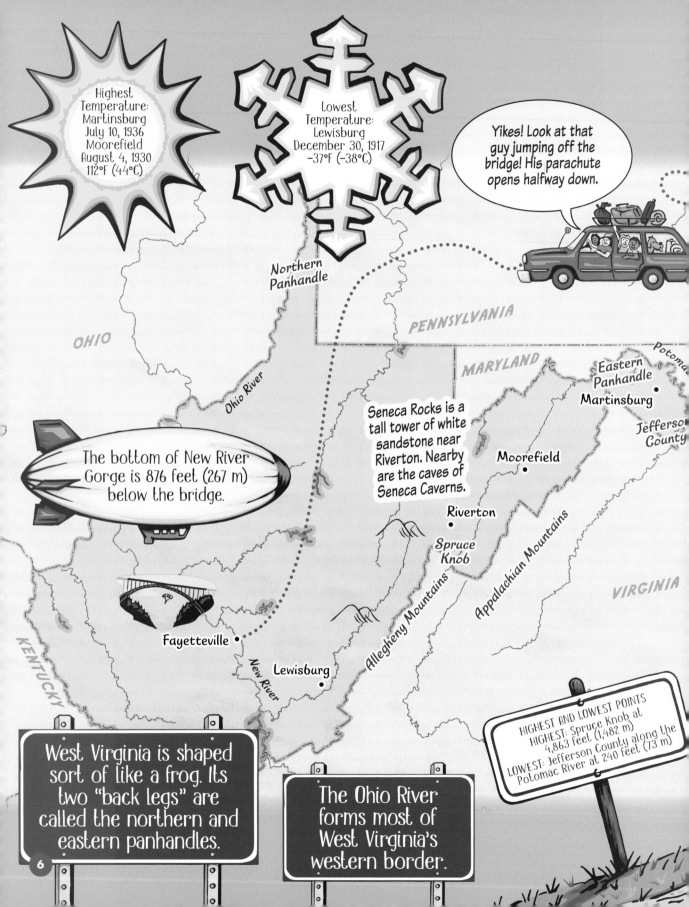

Highest Temperature:
Martinsburg
July 10, 1936
Moorefield
August 4, 1930
112°F (44°C)

Lowest Temperature:
Lewisburg
December 30, 1917
−37°F (−38°C)

Yikes! Look at that guy jumping off the bridge! His parachute opens halfway down.

Northern Panhandle

PENNSYLVANIA

OHIO

MARYLAND

Ohio River

Eastern Panhandle

Potoma

Martinsburg

Jefferso County

Seneca Rocks is a tall tower of white sandstone near Riverton. Nearby are the caves of Seneca Caverns.

Moorefield

The bottom of New River Gorge is 876 feet (267 m) below the bridge.

Riverton

Spruce Knob

Appalachian Mountains

VIRGINIA

Allegheny Mountains

KENTUCKY

Fayetteville

New River

Lewisburg

West Virginia is shaped sort of like a frog. Its two "back legs" are called the northern and eastern panhandles.

The Ohio River forms most of West Virginia's western border.

HIGHEST AND LOWEST POINTS
HIGHEST: Spruce Knob at 4,863 feet (1,482 m)
LOWEST: Jefferson County along the Potomac River at 240 feet (73 m)

BRIDGE DAY AT NEW RIVER GORGE

You're standing on a tall bridge. There's a river far below. You're probably gripping tightly to the railing. But dozens of people are leaping off the bridge!

What's going on here? It's Bridge Day in Fayetteville's New River Gorge! People parachute or **rappel** to the bottom. Not just anyone can do it, though. The jumpers have to be skilled and experienced.

The New River cuts through mountains. Mountains cover much of West Virginia. The Appalachian Mountains are in the east. The Allegheny Mountains are part of this area. To the west are steep hills and valleys. Many rivers and streams rush through the mountains.

A parachutist soars over New River Gorge on Bridge Day.

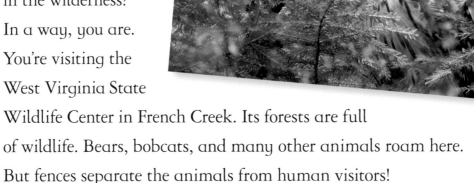

Wander along the wooded trails. Suddenly, you're face to face with a bear!

Are you deep in the wilderness? In a way, you are. You're visiting the West Virginia State Wildlife Center in French Creek. Its forests are full of wildlife. Bears, bobcats, and many other animals roam here. But fences separate the animals from human visitors!

Forests cover most of West Virginia. They make a great home for wild animals. Deer and bears live there. So do foxes, skunks, and raccoons. Chipmunks and rabbits scurry through the leaves. They're looking for nuts, grains, or berries.

You'll see owls, bears, and many kinds of animals at the West Virginia State Wildlife Center.

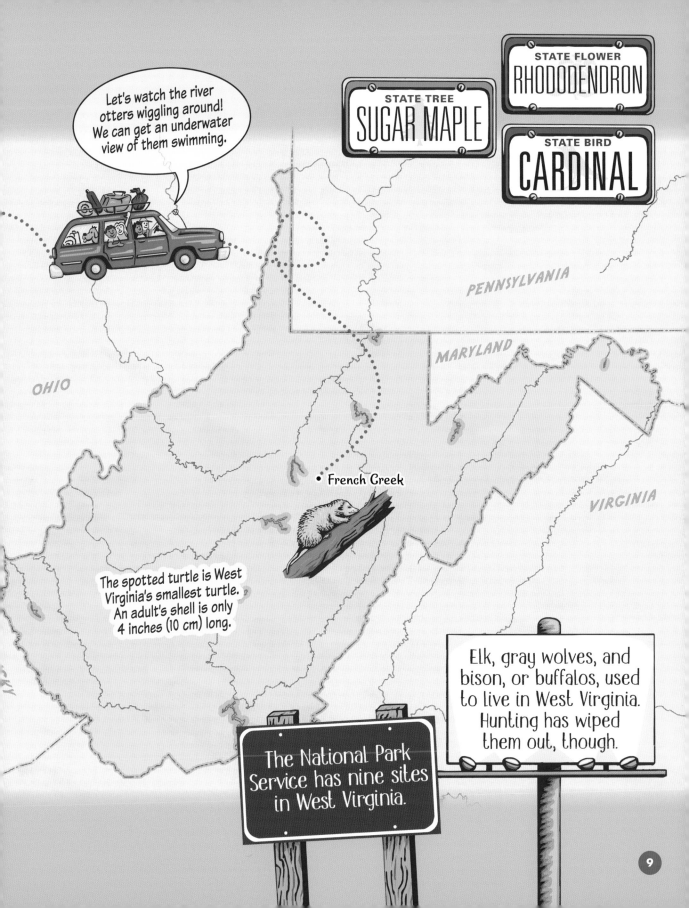

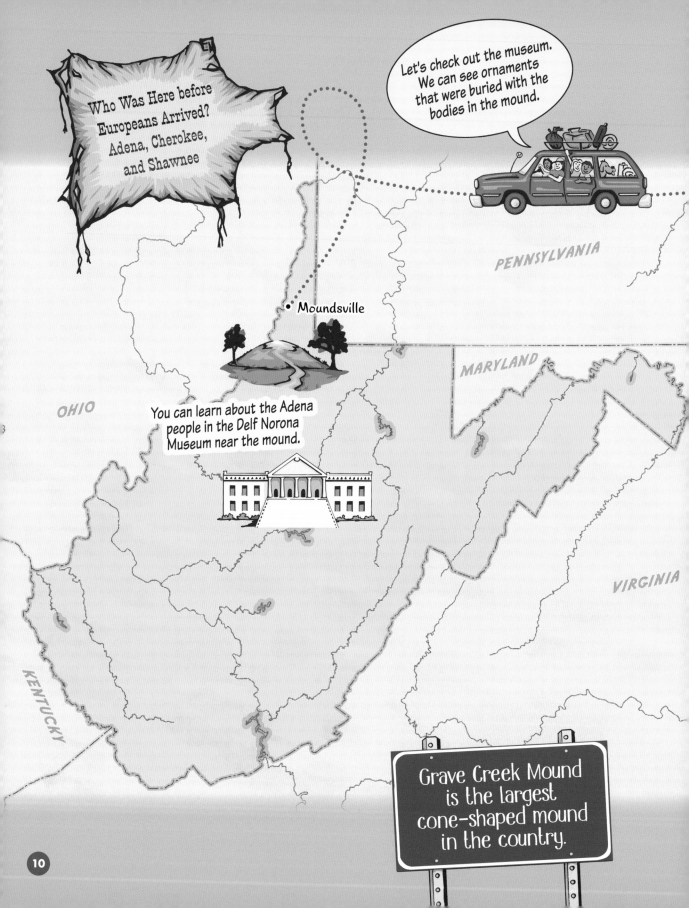

Who Was Here before Europeans Arrived? Adena, Cherokee, and Shawnee

Let's check out the museum. We can see ornaments that were buried with the bodies in the mound.

PENNSYLVANIA

• Moundsville

MARYLAND

OHIO

You can learn about the Adena people in the Delf Norona Museum near the mound.

VIRGINIA

KENTUCKY

Grave Creek Mound is the largest cone-shaped mound in the country.

GRAVE CREEK MOUND IN MOUNDSVILLE

It looks like a cone-shaped hill. But it was made by humans. It's Grave Creek Mound in Moundsville. The Adena people built it about 2,000 years ago. They piled up tons of earth. They buried many of their dead inside.

Several other Native American groups arrived after the Adena. Some were farmers. Others were hunters. In the 1600s, the Iroquois became very powerful. They tried to control the area. They wanted to hunt fur-bearing animals there. They traded the furs to Europeans.

European settlers arrived in about 1730. At that point, some Native American groups still lived in the area.

More than 3,500 Native Americans live in West Virginia today. Many belong to the Appalachian Cherokee Nation.

Grave Creek Mound dates back thousands of years.

PRICKETT'S FORT NEAR FAIRMONT

Step back in history at Prickett's Fort near Fairmont. People are spinning yarn and weaving cloth. Some are cooking in big kettles. There are blacksmiths and gunmakers, too.

This fort was first built in the 1700s. Now costumed workers are busy there. They show you how West Virginia **pioneers** lived.

English settlers established the Virginia **Colony** in 1607. It included land that is now West Virginia. At first, no European settlers moved that far west. Pioneers first came in the 1700s.

Most pioneers lived as farmers. They often clashed with Native Americans in the area. They fought over who had rights to the land. Settlers built many forts to defend themselves. One was Prickett's Fort.

Learn more about pioneer life when you visit Prickett's Fort State Park.

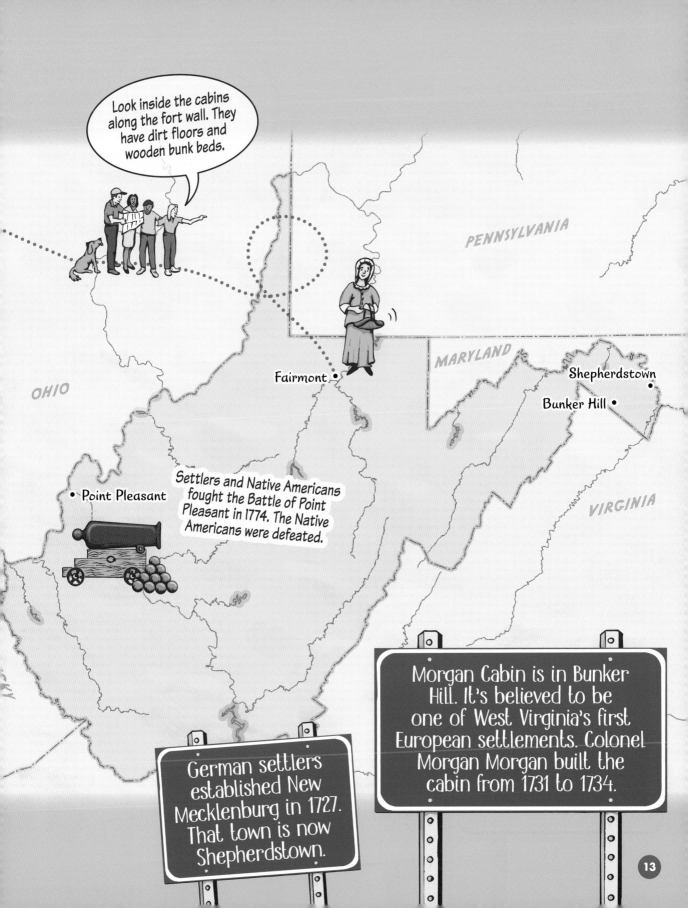

Look inside the cabins along the fort wall. They have dirt floors and wooden bunk beds.

PENNSYLVANIA

MARYLAND

OHIO

Fairmont

Shepherdstown

Bunker Hill

Point Pleasant

Settlers and Native Americans fought the Battle of Point Pleasant in 1774. The Native Americans were defeated.

VIRGINIA

Morgan Cabin is in Bunker Hill. It's believed to be one of West Virginia's first European settlements. Colonel Morgan Morgan built the cabin from 1731 to 1734.

German settlers established New Mecklenburg in 1727. That town is now Shepherdstown.

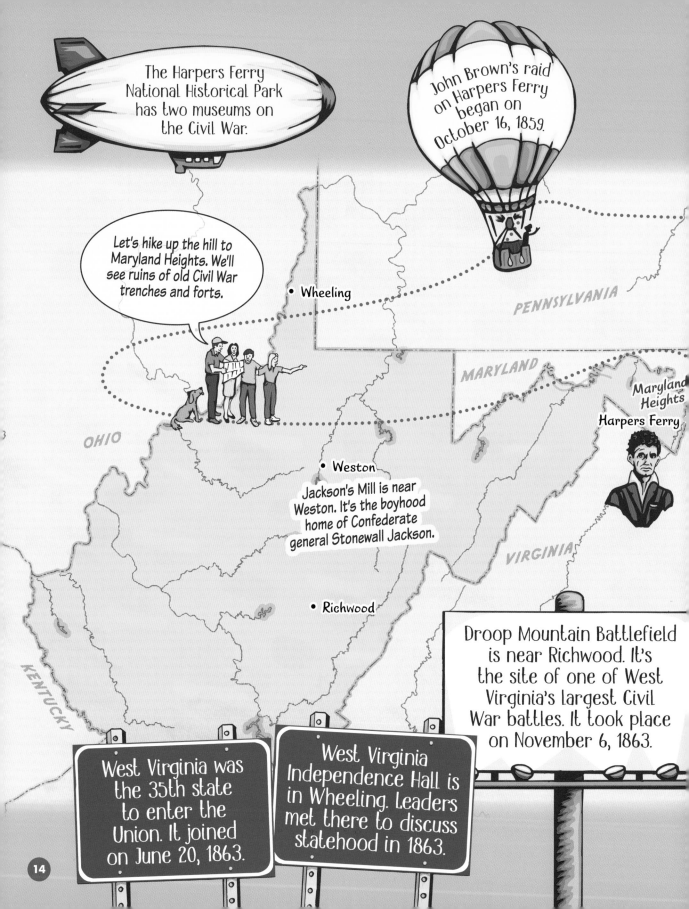

The Harpers Ferry National Historical Park has two museums on the Civil War.

John Brown's raid on Harpers Ferry began on October 16, 1859.

Let's hike up the hill to Maryland Heights. We'll see ruins of old Civil War trenches and forts.

• Wheeling

PENNSYLVANIA

MARYLAND

Maryland Heights

Harpers Ferry

OHIO

• Weston

Jackson's Mill is near Weston. It's the boyhood home of Confederate general Stonewall Jackson.

VIRGINIA

• Richwood

Droop Mountain Battlefield is near Richwood. It's the site of one of West Virginia's largest Civil War battles. It took place on November 6, 1863.

KENTUCKY

West Virginia was the 35th state to enter the Union. It joined on June 20, 1863.

West Virginia Independence Hall is in Wheeling. Leaders met there to discuss statehood in 1863.

HARPERS FERRY AND THE CIVIL WAR

One night in 1859, John Brown and a group of his supporters sneaked into Harpers Ferry. They raided a government **arsenal**. They hoped to steal thousands of guns. Brown wanted to use the guns to free enslaved African Americans. Brown's plan failed. He and six of his supporters were caught and killed. But his raid stirred up people's feelings. It helped lead to the Civil War (1861–1865).

The states fought this war over slavery. The Northern, or Union, side opposed slavery. Southern, or Confederate, states wanted to keep slavery.

Virginia joined the Confederacy. But many western Virginians opposed slavery. They formed the state of West Virginia and joined the Union. The Union won the war.

John Brown and his supporters took refuge in this guardhouse during their raid in Harpers Ferry.

BECKLEY EXHIBITION COAL MINE

Climb into the creaky train car. You're heading deep underground. There you'll wind through dark tunnels.

You're exploring Beckley Exhibition Coal Mine. And your guide is a real coal miner. He explains how miners used to work there.

Most parts of West Virginia contain coal. The mineral was first discovered there in 1742. Thousands of miners were working by the 1890s. They mined the coal with picks and shovels. It was dirty and dangerous work. Sometimes miners died in mine explosions.

By 1900, coal mining was the state's biggest **industry**. Coal helped other industries, too. Factories burned the coal in their furnaces.

Would you make a good miner? Tour Beckley Exhibition Coal Mine to find out!

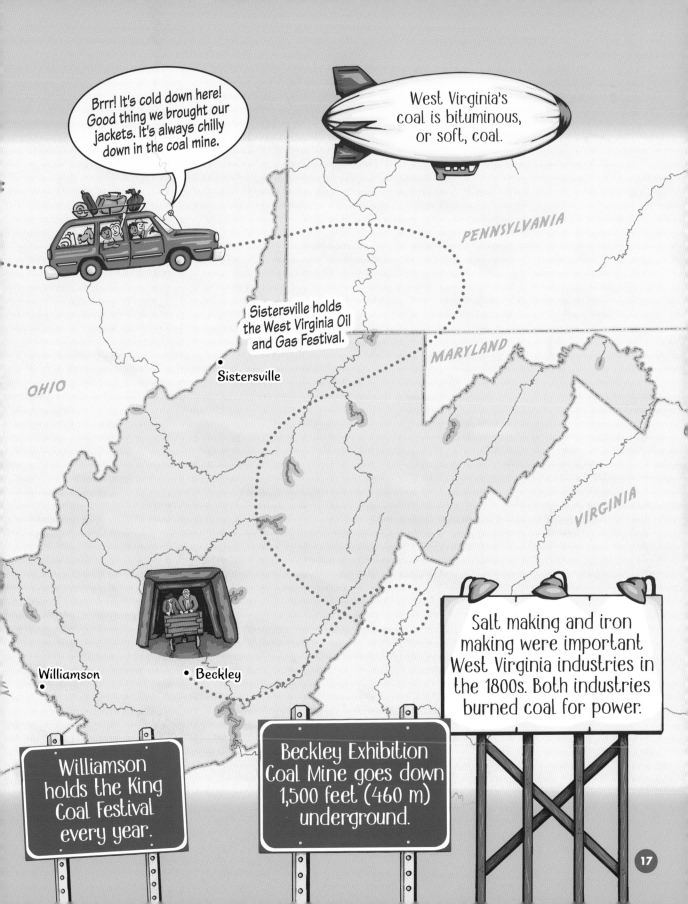

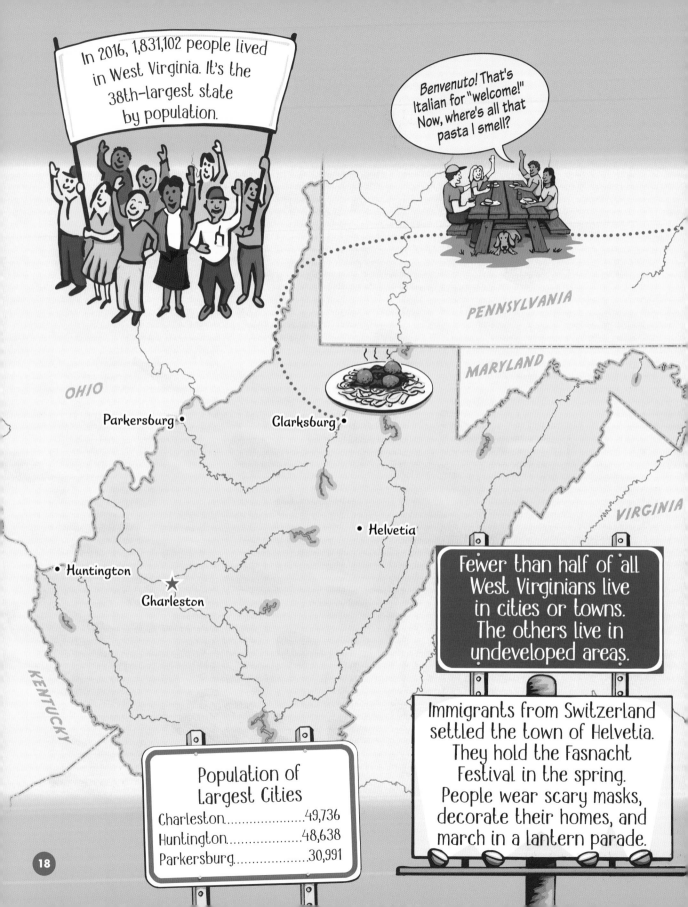

In 2016, 1,831,102 people lived in West Virginia. It's the 38th-largest state by population.

Benvenuto! That's Italian for "welcome!" Now, where's all that pasta I smell?

PENNSYLVANIA

MARYLAND

OHIO

Parkersburg •

Clarksburg •

VIRGINIA

• Helvetia

• Huntington

☆
Charleston

KENTUCKY

Fewer than half of all West Virginians live in cities or towns. The others live in undeveloped areas.

Population of Largest Cities

Charleston	49,736
Huntington	48,638
Parkersburg	30,991

Immigrants from Switzerland settled the town of Helvetia. They hold the Fasnacht Festival in the spring. People wear scary masks, decorate their homes, and march in a lantern parade.

CLARKSBURG'S ITALIAN HERITAGE FESTIVAL

Do you like pasta? Want to enter a hot-pepper-eating contest? Then come to the Italian Heritage Festival in Clarksburg! You'll be swept up in lively Italian music. And you'll eat your fill of Italian food!

Italians are among West Virginia's many **ethnic** groups. Many Italians arrived in the late 1800s. They came to work in the coal mines.

Other **immigrants** came from Poland, Germany, or Hungary. Some worked in the coal and lumber industries. Others worked in factories. Many groups still celebrate their **cultures** today.

Women wait to see who will be crowned queen of the Italian Heritage Festival in Clarksburg.

CASS SCENIC RAILROAD

Toot toot! All aboard! You're riding Cass Scenic Railroad. The train churns and clanks through the mountains. Thick black smoke belches from the smokestack.

At last, you get off at Whittaker Station near Cass. It's built like a 1940s logging camp. There you'll see the loggers' homes, tools, and machines.

Logging became a big industry in West Virginia. **Lumberjacks** cut down thousands of trees. Horses or trains hauled the logs away. Sawmills sawed the logs into boards. Cass was an important logging town. Most residents worked in its mills or lumber camps.

Want to ride the rails? Hop aboard a train at Cass!

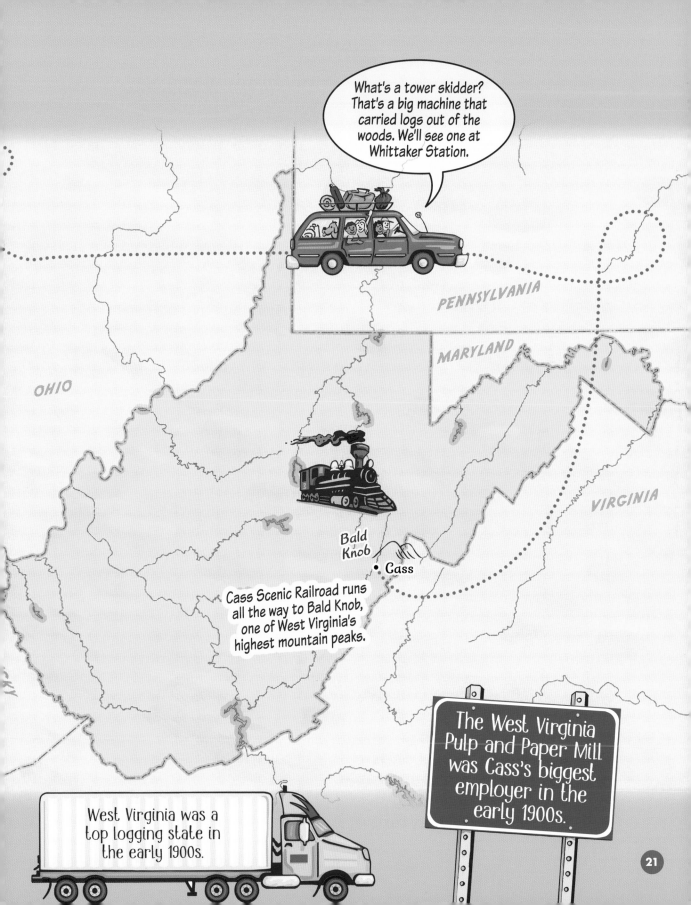

What's a tower skidder? That's a big machine that carried logs out of the woods. We'll see one at Whittaker Station.

PENNSYLVANIA

MARYLAND

OHIO

VIRGINIA

Bald Knob

• Cass

Cass Scenic Railroad runs all the way to Bald Knob, one of West Virginia's highest mountain peaks.

The West Virginia Pulp and Paper Mill was Cass's biggest employer in the early 1900s.

West Virginia was a top logging state in the early 1900s.

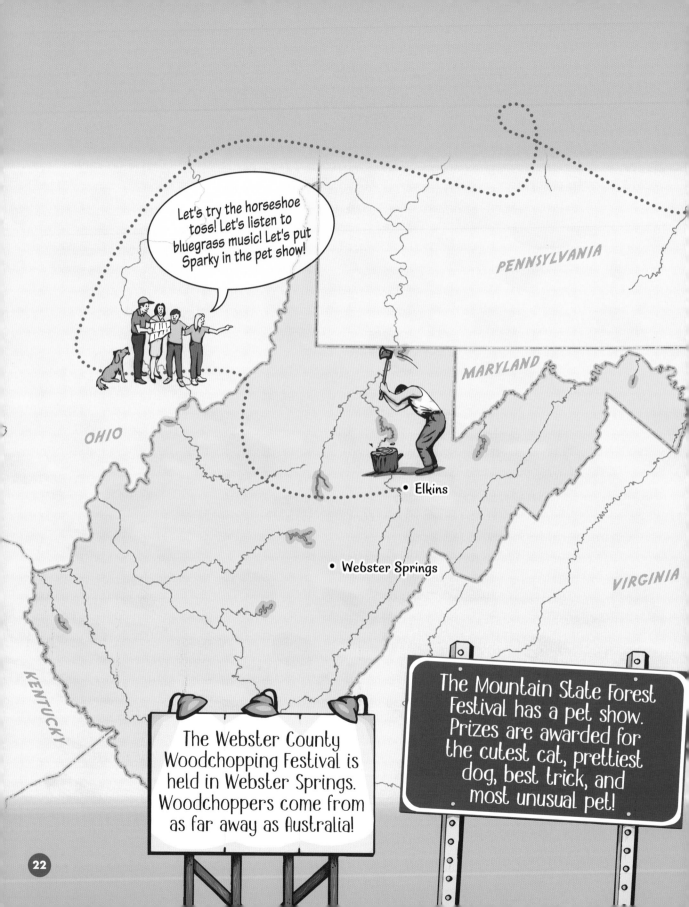

THE MOUNTAIN STATE FOREST FESTIVAL IN ELKINS

Lumberjacks compete in wood-chopping contests. Artists carve designs into wood. Men and women test their strength in weightlifting competitions. You're at the Mountain State Forest Festival in Elkins!

This festival celebrates West Virginia's lumber history. It also celebrates the skills needed to survive in the forest.

European settlers made their way into the forested mountains. They worked hard to make homes there. They chopped down trees and sawed them apart. They built their houses with the logs. Sometimes they hunted with bows and arrows. They had to be tough to stay alive!

Ready, set, chop! You'll see many wood-chopping contests at the Mountain State Forest Festival.

STUDYING SPACE AT THE GREEN BANK OBSERVATORY

Are you curious about outer space? Do you wonder what's out there? Just visit the Green Bank Observatory. You'll see a gigantic radio telescope. It's shaped like a big dish. Scientists use it to study space.

What's a radio telescope? Well, a regular telescope is like your eyes. It takes in light waves. But a radio telescope takes in radio waves. Where do the radio waves come from? Objects in space give them off.

Radio telescopes "see" things that regular telescopes can't. For example, they can observe exploded stars. This helps scientists discover the secrets of the universe!

Want to learn about the universe? Check out the radio telescope in Green Bank!

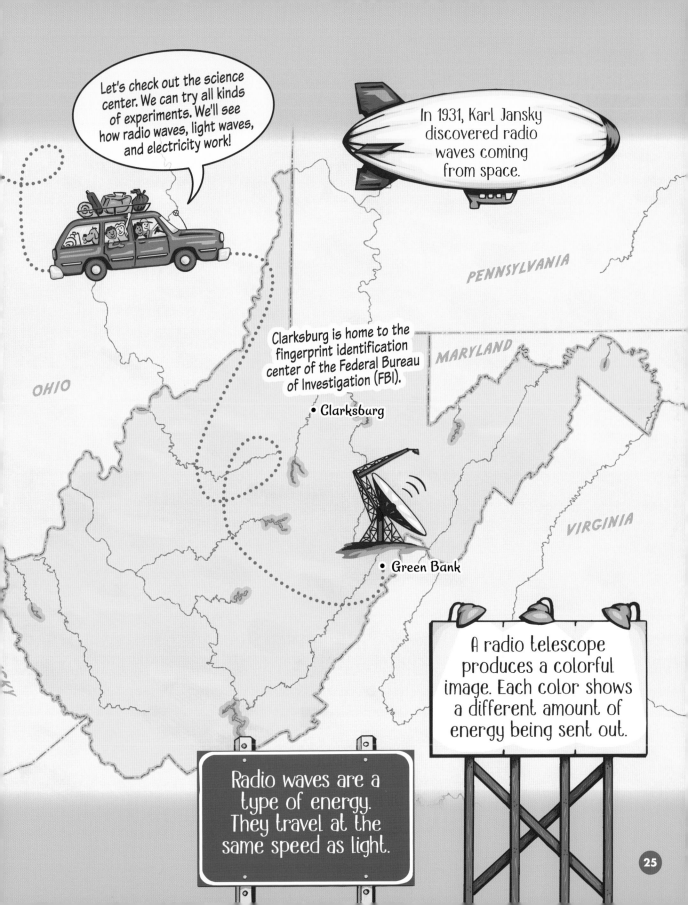

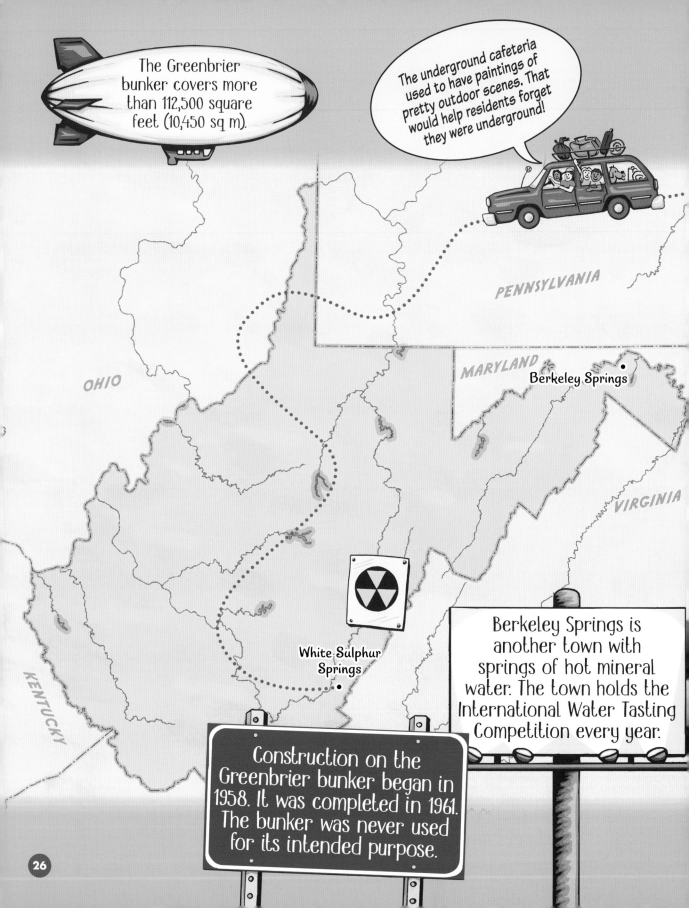

The Greenbrier bunker covers more than 112,500 square feet (10,450 sq m).

The underground cafeteria used to have paintings of pretty outdoor scenes. That would help residents forget they were underground!

PENNSYLVANIA

OHIO

MARYLAND

Berkeley Springs

VIRGINIA

White Sulphur Springs

KENTUCKY

Berkeley Springs is another town with springs of hot mineral water. The town holds the International Water Tasting Competition every year.

Construction on the Greenbrier bunker began in 1958. It was completed in 1961. The bunker was never used for its intended purpose.

Stroll into the elegant Greenbrier Hotel in White Sulphur Springs. People have come to this location since 1778. Its hot mineral waters are very healthful.

You can come and soak in the waters, too. You can also take a strange tour. You'll visit the hotel's underground bunker, or shelter. It has a cafeteria, recreation room, and hospital. Bunk beds fill the sleeping area. People could live here for months!

That was the idea. The U.S. government built this bunker. It could be used in case of war. Members of Congress would be able to live there safely. The shelter was closed in 1995. Now it gives visitors a peek into history.

Want to stay at a fancy hotel in West Virginia? Look no further than the Greenbrier Hotel!

Lots of state capitols have a dome. Only a few have a *golden* dome, though. One is West Virginia's capitol in Charleston. Its gold-coated dome glistens in the sunlight!

The state capitol overlooks the Kanawha River. Its shiny dome can be seen for miles.

Inside the capitol are state government offices. The state legislature meets here. It's the lawmaking branch of the state government. The governor heads another branch. This branch's job is to carry out the laws. Judges make up the third branch of the government. They decide whether someone has broken the law.

Lawmakers are busy inside the capitol in Charleston.

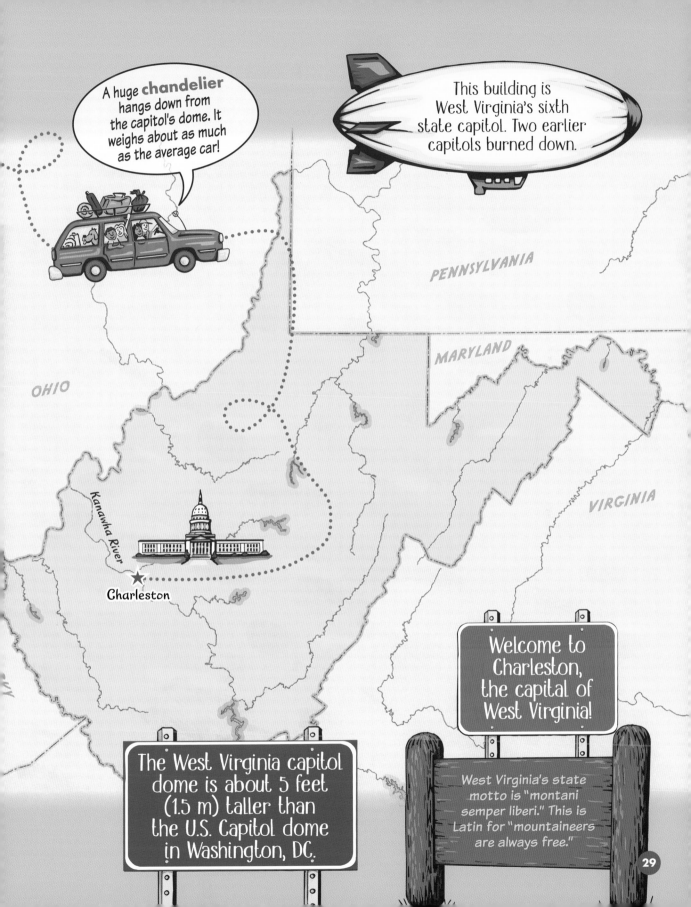

A huge **chandelier** hangs down from the capitol's dome. It weighs about as much as the average car!

This building is West Virginia's sixth state capitol. Two earlier capitols burned down.

PENNSYLVANIA

MARYLAND

OHIO

VIRGINIA

Kanawha River

★ Charleston

Welcome to Charleston, the capital of West Virginia!

West Virginia's state motto is "montani semper liberi." This is Latin for "mountaineers are always free."

The West Virginia capitol dome is about 5 feet (1.5 m) taller than the U.S. Capitol dome in Washington, DC.

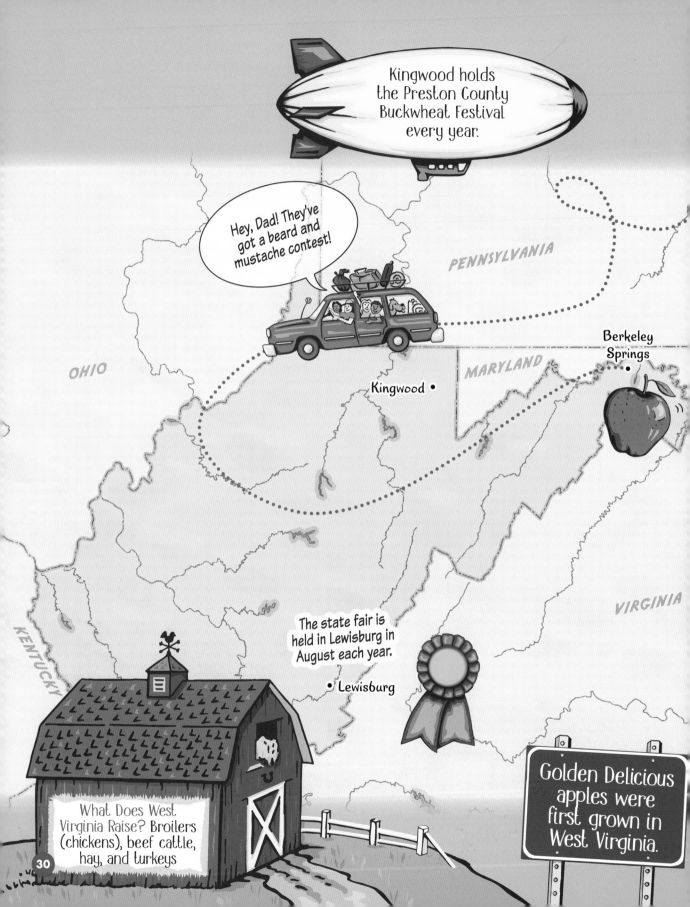

THE APPLE BUTTER FESTIVAL IN BERKELEY SPRINGS

Do you have a speedy turtle? Then enter it in the turtle race. Are you good at tossing eggs? How about calling hogs? You can enter contests for those skills, too.

You're at the Apple Butter Festival in Berkeley Springs! Sniff the air while you're there. You'll smell old-fashioned apple butter. People at the festival make it all day.

Eastern West Virginia is a big apple-growing region. Animals are the state's top farm products, though. Chickens and beef cattle are the most valuable. Hay is West Virginia's leading crop. Most of it ends up as cattle feed.

Are apples your favorite fruit? Then West Virginia's the state for you!

BLENKO GLASS COMPANY IN MILTON

A worker leans over the super-hot furnace. He gathers a gob of melted glass. The blower blows the gob into a shape. Then the finisher adds handles. Finally, there's a beautiful glass vase!

You're watching workers at Blenko Glass Company in Milton. West Virginia is famous for its glass products. Glass factories create bottles, stained glass, and windows. They make both useful and decorative glassware.

Chemicals are the state's top factory goods. Many chemicals are made from West Virginia's minerals. Those minerals include coal, natural gas, oil, and salt. Many factories also make metal or wood products.

A worker makes a glass vase at Blenko Glass Company.

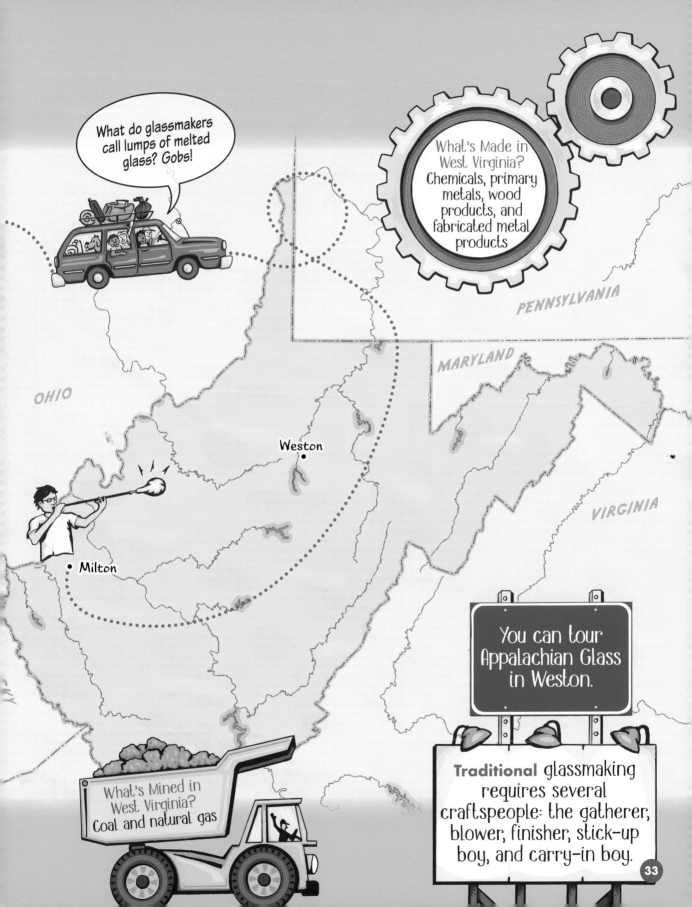

What do glassmakers call lumps of melted glass? Gobs!

What's Made in West Virginia?
Chemicals, primary metals, wood products, and fabricated metal products

PENNSYLVANIA

MARYLAND

OHIO

Weston

VIRGINIA

Milton

You can tour Appalachian Glass in Weston.

What's Mined in West Virginia?
Coal and natural gas

Traditional glassmaking requires several craftspeople: the gatherer, blower, finisher, stick-up boy, and carry-in boy.

33

Subscription libraries opened in Wheeling in 1807. Public libraries were not common until after 1900.

Let's compete in the spelling bee! They take the words from a McGuffey's Reader. Kids used that book in the 1800s.

PENNSYLVANIA

MARYLAND

OHIO

• Wheeling

• Glenville

• Ripley

Appalachian Mountains

VIRGINIA

★
Charleston

Allegheny Mountains

KENTUCKY

The Clay Center for the Arts and Sciences in Charleston features both art and science exhibits.

The Vandalia Gathering takes place in Charleston. It features Appalachian fiddling, dancing, storytelling, and crafts.

Ripley holds the Mountain State Art and Craft Fair in September.

THE FOLK FESTIVAL IN GLENVILLE

Kick up your heels to a fiddle tune. Watch a wood-carver hand-carve a bird. Then gobble up some beans and cornbread. You're enjoying the West Virginia State Folk Festival in Glenville!

This festival celebrates traditions of the Appalachian Region. People there developed many arts and crafts.

Today, the mountains are great for outdoor fun. People camp, hike, and watch wildlife there. In winter, people ski in the Allegheny Mountains. West Virginia's rivers attract lots of visitors, too. They drift downstream in kayaks or canoes. What a great escape!

Folk music is popular in West Virginia.

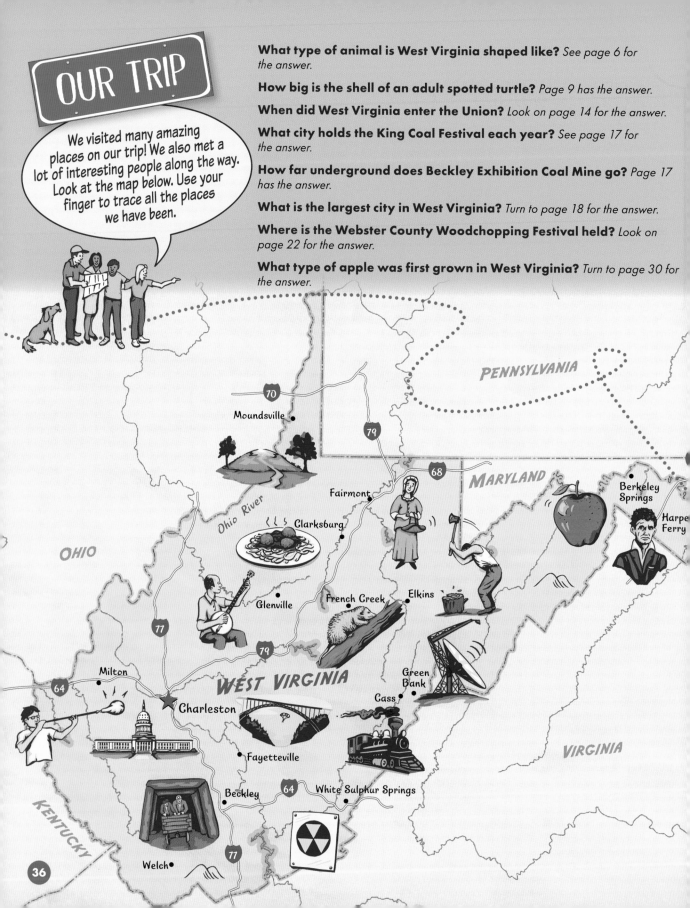

OUR TRIP

We visited many amazing places on our trip! We also met a lot of interesting people along the way. Look at the map below. Use your finger to trace all the places we have been.

What type of animal is West Virginia shaped like? *See page 6 for the answer.*

How big is the shell of an adult spotted turtle? *Page 9 has the answer.*

When did West Virginia enter the Union? *Look on page 14 for the answer.*

What city holds the King Coal Festival each year? *See page 17 for the answer.*

How far underground does Beckley Exhibition Coal Mine go? *Page 17 has the answer.*

What is the largest city in West Virginia? *Turn to page 18 for the answer.*

Where is the Webster County Woodchopping Festival held? *Look on page 22 for the answer.*

What type of apple was first grown in West Virginia? *Turn to page 30 for the answer.*

STATE SYMBOLS

State animal: Black bear

State bird: Cardinal

State butterfly: Monarch butterfly

State colors: Old gold and blue

State fish: Brook trout

State flower: Rhododendron (great laurel)

State fruit: Golden Delicious apple

State insect: Honeybee

State soil: Monongahela silt loam

State tree: Sugar maple

State seal

STATE SONG

"THE WEST VIRGINIA HILLS"
Words by Ellen King, music by H. E. Engle

Oh, the West Virginia hills!
How majestic and how grand,
With their summits bathed in glory,
Like our Prince Immanuel's land!
Is it any wonder then,
That my heart with rapture thrills,
As I stand once more with loved ones
On these West Virginia hills?

Chorus:
O the hills, Beautiful hills,
How I love those West Virginia hills.
If o'er sea or land I roam
Still I think of happy home
And the friends among the West
Virginia hills.

Oh, the West Virginia hills!
Where my childhood hours
    were passed,
Where I often wandered lonely,
And the future tried to cast;
Many are our visions bright,
Which the future ne'er fulfills;

But how sunny were my daydreams
On those West Virginia hills!
(Chorus)

Oh, the West Virginia hills! How
unchang'd they seem to stand,
With their summits pointed skyward
To the Great Almighty's Land!
Many changes I can see,
Which my heart with sadness fills;
But no changes can be noticed
In those West Virginia hills.

(Chorus)

Oh, the West Virginia hills!
I must bid you now adieu.
In my home beyond the mountains
I shall ever dream of you;
In the evening time of life,
If my Father only wills,
I shall still behold the vision
Of those West Virginia hills.

(Chorus)

That was a great trip! We have traveled all over West Virginia! There are a few places that we didn't have time for, though. Next time, we plan to visit the Kimball War Memorial in Welch. The memorial was built in 1928. It honors African Americans who fought bravely during World War I.

FAMOUS PEOPLE

Brett, George (1953–), baseball player

Buck, Pearl S. (1892–1973), author

Dru, Joanne (1922–1996), actor

Harvey, Steve (1957–), TV host and actor

Jackson, Thomas J. "Stonewall" (1824–1863), Confederate general

Knight, John S. (1894–1981), journalist and publisher

Knotts, Don (1924–2006), actor

Knowles, John (1926–2001), author

Martin, Christy (1968–), boxer

Nash, John Forbes, Jr. (1928–2015), mathematician and Nobel Prize winner

Paisley, Brad (1972–), country music singer

Retton, Mary Lou (1968–) gymnast and Olympic gold medalist

Reuther, Walter (1907–1970), labor leader

Rylant, Cynthia (1954–), children's book author

Vance, Cyrus (1917–2002), public official

Washington, Booker T. (1856–1915), educator and founder of the Tuskegee Institute

West, Jerry (1938–), basketball player

Williams, Deron (1984–), basketball player

Woodson, Carter G. (1875–1950), educator and author

Yeager, Chuck (1923–), first person to fly faster than the speed of sound

WORDS TO KNOW

arsenal (AR-suh-nul) a storehouse for weapons

chandelier (shan-duh-LEER) a fancy light fixture that hangs down from the ceiling

colony (KOL-uh-nee) a land with ties to a mother country

cultures (KUHL-churz) the customs, beliefs, and ways of life of groups of people

ethnic (ETH-nik) having to do with a person's race or nationality

immigrants (IM-uh-gruhnts) people who move from their home country to another country

industry (IN-duh-stree) a type of business

lumberjacks (LUM-burr-jaks) people who cut trees down and saw them into logs

pioneers (py-uh-NEERZ) people who move to an unsettled land

rappel (ruh-PELL) to descend from a high place by sliding down a rope that's partly wrapped around the body

traditional (truh-DISH-uhn-ul) following long-held customs

State flag

TO LEARN MORE

IN THE LIBRARY

Byers, Ann. *West Virginia: Past and Present*. New York, NY: Rosen Central, 2011.

Hinton, Kaavonia. *The Iroquois of the Northeast*. Kennett Square, PA: Purple Toad, 2013.

Owings, Lisa. *West Virginia: The Mountain State*. Minneapolis, MN: Bellwether, 2014.

Stefoff, Rebecca. *John Brown and the Armed Resistance to Slavery*. New York, NY: Cavendish Square, 2016.

ON THE WEB
Visit our Web site for links about West Virginia:
childsworld.com/links

Note to Parents, Teachers, and Librarians: We routinely verify our Web links to make sure they are safe and active sites. So encourage your readers to check them out!

PLACES TO VISIT OR CONTACT
The West Virginia State Museum
wvculture.org
1900 Kanawha Boulevard East
Charleston, WV 25305
304/558-0220
For more information about the history of West Virginia

West Virginia Division of Tourism
gotowv.com
90 MacCorkle Ave SW
South Charleston, WV 25303
800/225-5982
For more information about traveling in West Virginia

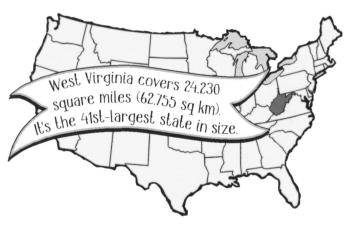

West Virginia covers 24,230 square miles (62,755 sq km). It's the 41st-largest state in size.

INDEX

Bye, Mountain State.
We had a great time.
We'll come back soon!